Lutheran Trump Cards

Playing Our Best Hand in the 21st Century

By Dave Daubert

Day 8 Strategies
Elgin, IL

© Copyright 2014 by David Dennison Daubert

All rights reserved. No part of this publication may be reproduced, distributed, or transmitted in any form or by any means, including photocopying, recording, or other electronic or mechanical methods, without the prior written permission of the publisher, except in the case of brief quotations embodied in critical reviews and certain other uses permitted by copyright law. For permission requests, write to the publisher, addressed "Attention: Permissions Coordinator," at the address below.

Larger quantities of this book are available at a discount. For information on purchasing for orders larger than 10 copies, contact the publisher at Resources@Day8Strategies.com for more information.

ISBN 978-0-9910621-0-2

Day 8 Books
1132 Morningside Dr.
Elgin, IL 60123
www.Day8Strategies.com

To contact the author send an email to: Resources@Day8Strategies.com

Dedicated to everyone who has ever struggled to find the right words to say.

Table of Contents

Preface 7

Ace: There is no way to God (period) 13
King: Jesus reveals that God is love 17
Queen: Grace for us includes hope for others 21
Jack: All the baptized have a vocation 25
Ten: The priesthood of all believers 29
Nine: Life is sacramental 33
Eight: Worship is horizontal 37
Seven: Love the Bible without worshiping it 41
Six: Perfection is not the point 45
Five: Respond with freedom and gratitude 49
Four: Faith forms the church 53
Three: We have an ecumenical heart 57
Two: We are always watching for change 61

Conclusion 65

Preface

As we approach the 500th anniversary of the Reformation, the premise of this book is that the work started by Luther and other evangelical reformers is of lasting value. The word "evangelical" at that time referred to the sense that the reforms were bringing "good news" to the people – and was not as narrow a term as it has become in some corners of the American church today. At the heart of this book is the belief that there is something at the core of the movement that has become known as "Lutheran" that is worth thinking about in the 21st century.

Recent studies about the place of religion in North America show an ongoing decline in interest and commitment to the church as a place for people to live out their spiritual journeys. More and more people are referring to themselves as "spiritual, but not religious." It is not that the majority of them has lost interest in God or has taken up atheism as a worldview. Quite the contrary, interest in spirituality may, in some ways, be higher than ever. But more and more people are not looking to organized religion for the answers to their spiritual questions.

Some of this is simply a decrease in interest in institutions of any form. "Joining" is down in more than just the church. In addition, various negative stories about the church and its monetary and sexual sins have made people increasingly skeptical of the church's claims, many of which are grounded in some sense of moral authority that the church seems to have lost. In a world with fast paced choices and highly engaging ways of communicating, many people are just bored with the seemingly endless drone of the routines in many churches.

Much of the work I do with church leaders involves interaction with leaders who claim the name "Lutheran." These leaders are usually concerned with either the quality of the leadership or the effectiveness of the congregations within the Lutheran Church. Inevitably, the topics of theology and discipleship come up again and again. How can we help people in our congregations be more energized and excited about their faith in what God has done in Jesus Christ? How can we revitalize congregations to be spiritually more helpful to people? If God is active and at work in the world, how can we help people individually, as well as congregations corporately, join in with God's work and make a real difference in the things that matter most? And, what do leaders need to know and do in order to help the people they work with and the congregations they lead work more effectively?

In talking about these issues, I naturally tend to use key points in Lutheran theology to help people see how the things we are working on are connected to the core of who they are as Lutherans. Often these ideas come up repeatedly in different settings. As they arise, I tell people, "We have to use that idea. It's one of our trump cards." It is a phrase I find myself repeating again and again in different places. Over time, it became more and more clear that there were key ideas that seemed essential to our identity as Lutheran Christians. The list began to emerge in my mind, and I found ways to use items from it again and again. There is great treasure in this Lutheran stuff, and many of us aren't quite sure what it is!

In his book, *A Generous Orthodoxy*, Brian McLaren says, "If you want a feel for the richness of the phrase 'Word of God,' ask the Lutherans; it's a secret that their own tradition seems to know without knowing what it means"(Zondervan/Youth Specialties, 2006, p. 163). This is telling; people see wonderful insights in our teaching, and glimpse things that are really helpful. But somehow, many of us have simply taken these things for granted and have lost sight of our own unique insights. Others among us know that, at some basic level, they semi-remember things from their confirmation classes years ago, but have no way of using or making sense of them today. If these great things are there for us, how can we discern them, and make them fresh and useful again?

This little book is an attempt to help bring these core ideas out into the open, making them clear and available to people again. The face cards—Ace, King, Queen and Jack—provide enough for any person to find help in their own faith journey, as well as guiding others in their spiritual quests. An article I wrote for *The Lutheran* magazine in October 2013 used the face cards as a starting point for people to reflect on the strengths of Lutheran faith. As part of writing that article, Elizabeth Hunter on *The Lutheran* staff asked me about the rest of the cards in our Lutheran suit. She believed that seeing the face cards would make people wonder about the rest of the cards in our hand. I had been blogging about these a few months earlier, and had many of these "trump cards" defined. Liz's request made me decide to finish the suit: a full set of cards from the Two all the way up to the Ace.

Each chapter focuses on one point, and contains a witnessing idea, which uses that point to shape how we think and talk about what we believe. There are also questions for reflection or discussion, so this book could be useful to an individual, or used with a group. There is, at least in my mind, a flow to the book. The chapters build on each other, or connect to the previous ones, in some meaningful way.

You will also notice the graphics for the cards in each chapter are based on the hearts in a regular deck. At the same time, they are different; these hearts have a cross in the center. This is the heart that rests in the center of Luther's Rose, a graphic developed by Luther himself to remind people of the basics of the faith in a world where not everyone could read. Luther saw the dark cross as the center, marking the death of Jesus as the center of our message. The heart around it was not dead though, but bright red and full of life, a gift given by the same Jesus of the cross. Around these is the rose, its petals white, as signs of grace and forgiveness that wash us clean. The petals rest in a background of blue, the color of hope, something all Christians possess, as we trust in the God of Jesus. Finally, around the outside is a ring of gold, representing the life eternal that Christ gives, as well as the lasting and most precious gift offered. While the whole image would be cumbersome on playing cards, the hearts with the cross at the center should remind us all that the core of Lutheran teaching is always an encounter with the Jesus who went to the cross and arose from the dead. That encounter is to bring life to us, not death.

Some points on the list in this book originated in Lutheran teaching, but may be in other traditions' teaching as well. Those traditions have received them from us as a part of the Lutheran contribution to the thinking of the wider church. Other ideas have been inherited from pre-Reformation teachings, and have clear roots in the Roman Catholic Church, but have then evolved, or been intentionally shaped, to be distinctly Lutheran in some way. I see both the individual ideas, and the framework they create, as being "Lutheran."

Like any interpretive effort, this book has a personal "spin" on these ideas. That spin is impacted by the fact that I am a part of the Evangelical Lutheran Church in America, and not in one of the other strands of Lutheranism in North America. Also, I have spent much of my professional career working on leadership and organizational change for the sake of joining in with God's mission to love and bless the world. I see doctrine as both rooted in the tradition, and open to transformation. Doctrines that are not rooted seem to lack grounding for lasting use and leave us wanting something deeper. Doctrines that are too static tend to hang on long past their usefulness and eventually suck the life out of us.

Somehow, in the reframing and reconnecting of core teachings with fresh uses and interpretations, traditions manage to keep themselves alive and maintain the ability to be useful. This little book is an attempt to claim and reframe things at the heart of Lutheran teaching: our very best stuff. Much of it will be familiar (I hope) but perhaps phrased in a way that helps you think of something in a fresh way. Some of it may seem new to you, but in a way that, when you think about it, you are able to own and say "amen" to. Ultimately, this is not a systematic theology to make us all academically smarter, but a conversation starter to get us all thinking, talking and living out our faith in ways that are relevant and matter in our lives.

Finally, this book is intended to generate thought and dialog. The end of each chapter has scripture passages to read and reflect about in the light of the theme of the chapter from a biblical perspective. There are also a few questions for discussion or reflection. If you are reading this alone, you may be blessed by taking a little time to journal on the questions after reading a chapter. If you are reading this with others, using the questions as a jumping off point for discussion should give you a chance to learn from others and share ideas and support.

The chapters that follow lead you from the ace through to the two in the Lutheran suit. Let's begin!

The Ace
There is No Way to God (Period)

I first noticed a need for attention to the items in this series of trump cards while I was teaching at a pastors' theological conference. I was doing a piece on some of the most unique insights of Lutheranism and how these ideas were helpful in our work to share our faith and walk with people through life's struggles.

I was making a statement about some other Christian faith traditions and how they view the connection between God and people. I said, "Many traditions in our country teach that there is no way to God except through Jesus Christ." The reason for this was to counter this point with the subject of this chapter—there is no way to God (Period). But, before I caught my breath and left a little pause to bring my point home, a pastor in the crowd said, "Amen. That's right."

I had not expected that response. These were all church professionals and every one of them worked in the Lutheran Church. They had seminary degrees. If anyone would understand the points I was going to make that morning, surely this group would. So an "Amen" to something I was planning to counter was not what I had expected. It felt a little awkward!

And so I stopped and responded to the pastor. "No," I said, "That's not right. That's not what we teach. We teach that there is no way to God—period." I could sense a bit of a reaction. I had hit a nerve and for the most part, people seemed excited by it. Then I proceeded to resume what I was going to share.

On the screen I put up a picture that many of us have seen in religious tracts over the years. People have hung them on our doors or handed them to us as they shared their understanding of the Christian faith and urged us to make a decision to accept Christ. In the picture there is a huge chasm, deep and wide. On one side of the chasm we see the word "God." On the other side we see the word "man." The explanation tells us that the chasm is caused by our sin and that it is too wide for us to cross. There is no way we can get to God on our own. But in the center of the chasm there is a picture of a cross. The arms of the cross reach across the chasm like a bridge. If we accept Christ and repent of our sins, Christ provides a way across to God. The picture shows a man scurrying across with an arrow by him to show him moving from the world of sin to enjoy eternal life with God.

Now, most Lutherans are pretty uncomfortable with this picture. On the conscious side, we don't like the sense that we have to make a decision to accept Christ to be with God. We Lutherans don't like "decision theology" at all. But I think there is also a more subconscious discomfort with the picture. We can't all name it. But it just doesn't feel like us. It isn't a picture we want to use.

Here is the reason: One of Luther's personal struggles was an obsession with getting life right so he would end up with God rather than be condemned. He tried to find peace in repenting and confessing but, as soon as he was done, he started to notice or remember things he had done but forgotten to confess. This literally drove him crazy and he could not find peace, no matter how he tried. Luther's great insight discovered this key truth—nothing we can do can get us right with God and no amount of effort on our part can get us to eternity. In this matter we are powerless.

On the surface this may not seem like a very good first card. You may be thinking, "Our best point is that there is no way to God? That sounds pretty negative and discouraging. We know so many people who are searching for God and trying to find their way. Can we really tell them to give it up, that there is simply no way to God at all—no exceptions?"

The Lutheran answer is to say, "Yes!" Tell them to give it up. The burden of trying to find a way to get to God, and finding a system or activity or status that makes it possible, is life draining. It causes many people to lament their inability to get there or make any progress in their spiritual journey. Nothing sucks the life out of someone more than the endless attempt to arrive at the impossible.

The kindest thing we can do is help people see that they don't need to get to God. The Christian message is grounded in a gospel where God always goes first, always initiates, and comes to us. Right from the beginning when God made the world and everything in it, and then came to walk with Adam and Eve in the garden that God had planted for them to till and cultivate. It happened when God came to Abraham and Sarah in the persons of three visitors and announced that they would have a son. It happened when Moses met God, who came to him in the burning bush and called him to lead God's people to freedom. It happened over and over again in God's story. It has always been this way. It continues to be this way. We don't have any way to get to God and, once we discover that, rather than working to figure out what will get us "there," we are freed to simply be "here" and watch for God's coming.

We'll explore this more in the next chapter when we look at grace, the content of our second card. But for now, it is enough to celebrate the news that we can stop trying to do the right thing or make the appropriate response so that we can get to God. Oddly, the first card calls us to the spiritual discipline of "relax," the pressure is off. Our ability to free people from the thought that there is some right way for them to find God is one of our greatest gifts. It's our "ace in the hole," and pretty unique in today's religious landscape where most groups have some way to help you find God (if only you just do it "right").

For Reflection or Discussion

Look at the following passages from the Bible and take some time to reflect or discuss how these texts relate to the idea that there is no way to God (period). Discuss this with others or spend time reflecting or journaling about your thoughts.

- » Psalm 22:1-2
- » Matthew 27:45-50

Take time to think about the following questions and then either journal personally about them or discuss them in a group:

- ♥ What did you think about this chapter? What point or points stand out about it most?
- ♥ When have you felt cut off from God? What did you experience and how did you feel?
- ♥ How do you feel when someone shows you some kind of step by step instructions on how you can "find God?" If you encounter such a situation again, what could you say that would be both helpful and gracious (not just a sharp tongued comeback line!)?
- ♥ If there is no way to get to God,
    - » What practices in your life help you to be more attentive and able to watch for the God who comes to you?
    - » How could you be more intentional about making time to wait, watch and listen?
    - » What help would you like from your faith community to be better equipped to watch for God?

The King
Jesus Reveals God is Love

In itself, the presence of God can either be good or bad news. Many early religions were grounded in appeasing the gods in order to keep something bad from happening. The idea was to discern how to appease the god or gods in question, which primarily raised anxiety. If the gods were not appeased, problems would come as a result. Early religions were often heavily grounded in ongoing rites of sacrifice. These ranged from offering livestock to human sacrifices.

The biblical story did not emerge without including this reality; human sacrifice was present in neighboring people groups. In Genesis 22, Abraham experiences a calling from God to offer his son Isaac as a sacrifice. While human sacrifice was acceptable in the world from which Judaism emerged, Judaism itself excluded human sacrifice, a fact that the story of Abraham and Isaac underscores, choosing, instead, to rely on animal sacrifices.

In Isaiah 6:1-8 we see Isaiah, one of God's great prophets, encounter God in the heart of the temple. This is not a place where people just went – it was viewed as way to dangerous to just wander in to check out the decorations and the architecture. The common understandings about God in Isaiah's time meant that face to face encounters with God were potentially life threatening and to be feared rather than to be desired. Rather than rejoicing that he is blessed to spend time with God, Isaiah quakes with fear, for he believes that encountering God is sure to result in certain harm and perhaps even lead to his death. He is not good enough to be there.

So we see that the idea that God can and does come to us is important—but it is not enough. Isaiah's instinctive fear when he finds himself in God's presence is a reminder that God's arrival is just as likely to be bad news as good. Until we are clear about who God is and what God is about, the fact that God comes to us can be just plain scary! What if God's coming to us is just as ominous as it was for Isaiah? Is the God who comes to us ultimately to be feared as someone who wants our destruction or to be welcomed as someone who wants us to live?

That brings us squarely to our second card in the Lutheran suit. Jesus reveals that God is love. For Lutheran Christians, that's why Jesus stands as the central figure in our faith.

In Jesus we discover the truth that God is love. This love is *costly,* as is shown in Jesus' willingness to suffer and die at the cross. And it is *persistent,* as is seen in the resurrection. Lutherans, this amazing encounter with love in the death and resurrection of Jesus is called the "theology of the cross." It is not only good news to discover God is not who we fear God could be, it is also that we meet God in the surprising place of the cross and in the death and resurrection of Jesus that shows us something that was hidden about God. This love is the content of grace, which is seen in the nature of Christ in how he brings forgiveness and new life. In spite of what we may do, God always comes back again. And that return is a new chance to begin new life.

Nowhere is this more evident than in the account of the resurrection in John 20:19-23. It is the first Easter Sunday and the disciples have heard from the women that Jesus' tomb is empty and that he has appeared to them—he is alive. That news, while unsettling enough, is mixed in with the reality that, as Jesus' disciples, they may be in danger of meeting the same fate as Jesus. Their hope is that if they wait things out long enough, locked together in a room, the furor over Jesus and his death will subside and they will be able to get out unscathed.

Into this fear-filled scene comes Jesus. Through locked doors he appears to this scared band of followers. Remember, this is a group of people who fled, lied and denied even knowing Jesus during the last twenty-four hours he was alive. Now he's back and you have to assume he's not too happy with their performance. And if they thought he was powerful before, now he has shown them that he can even come back from the dead.

He opens his arms to them and, in the midst of their fears, says, "Peace be with you." It is not too likely that this is what they were expecting to hear. John doesn't tell us their reaction or describe their faces, but we can pretty easily surmise that they were shocked. This is so important for Jesus to say, and for the disciples to hear, that he repeats himself. Again he says, "Peace be with you." His words, as heartfelt as they are, plow through all sorts of baggage for the disciples. In light of all that had happened, and how the disciples had responded, Jesus' coming back was an ambiguous event at best. What if he wanted revenge for their mistakes?

"Peace be with you," Jesus says again, "As the Father has sent me, so I send you. If you forgive the sins of any, they are forgiven. If you retain the sins of any, they are retained."

Not only does Jesus' return embody grace and love, it also calls for that same thing to issue forth from his disciples. Forgiveness for shortcomings is given. Peace is granted. Meaning and purpose and the chance to join in the work that Jesus is already doing are offered.

This is stating the obvious for many of us. But you need only watch the news, religious TV, the political alignment of various groups (especially many Christian ones) to know that many don't believe this. Many believe that God is just and judges first—loving primarily those who respond "correctly." While faith matters greatly to those who walk along the same path as we do, we know that faith does not make God love us—it helps us trust that God already does (no footnotes or exception clauses).

For Reflection or Discussion

Look at the following passages from the Bible and take some time to reflect or discuss how these texts relate to the idea that Jesus reveals that God is love. Discuss this with others or spend time reflecting or journaling about your thoughts.

- » Romans 8:31-39
- » John 1:14-18

Take time to think about the following questions and then either journal personally about them or discuss them in a group:

- ♥ What did you think about this chapter? What point or points stand out about it most?
- ♥ What does grace mean to you? How would you describe it to someone else?
- ♥ Where have you experienced genuine grace that came to you as a true gift? If you are doing this book with others, share the story to them.
- ♥ How do you understand the work of Jesus to be about grace? When you say, "Jesus reveals God is gracious…" in a way that is truly personal for you, what kinds of things would you include?

The Queen
Grace for Us Includes Hope for Others

In 2012, a gunman went to a movie theater in Aurora, CO, for the opening showing of the final movie in the Batman trilogy. He opened fire and made us all too painfully aware of how fragile human life is and how callously it can be treated. Although events like this are shocking, they are also all too common—we seem to find ourselves shocked again and again and again and...

But the response to events like this, from people who claim to be followers of Jesus, does continue to surprise me. Jerry Newcombe of the American Family Association, a "Christian" group that has lots of supporters and funding (and is also on the Southern Poverty Law Center's list of hate groups) came out with the following statement in response to the shootings:

> "If a Christian dies early, if a Christian dies young, it seems tragic, but really it is not tragic because they are going to a wonderful place. On the other hand, if a person doesn't know Jesus Christ... if they knowingly rejected Jesus Christ, then, basically, they are going to a terrible place."

(**www.HuffingtonPost.com**, July 22, 2012)

So, to be clear, the non-Christians who were shot in the theater are all now in hell, according the AFA's Jerry Newcombe.

When I showed this quote to a Lutheran friend and asked him what he thought, his response was, "I read this and it made me cringe." I couldn't agree more. It made me wonder what it was in our theological DNA as Lutherans that made us feel such sadness and distaste at something that someone else, who is also on some level claiming to also be a "Christian," held as a matter of obvious fact and even seemed to revel in.

When we are at our best and most clear about what we bring to the table, there is something in our core that will not allow us to pronounce ultimate judgment on someone else, no matter how easy (or desirable) it might seem to do so. This trait is not a new modern innovation; it lies in some of the roots of our Lutheran movement's early days when discussions with other reforming groups showed a clear difference of opinion on this matter.

The issue of who received grace and who didn't was a fundamental one among early Protestants. Even today, not all Christians (not even all Protestants) would agree with the above statement on who gets grace, how grace is received, or even what grace is. Some believe that if someone doesn't profess faith in Christ out loud, they are going to hell.

At the time of the Reformation, one controversy among Protestants was over the topic of "predestination." This was the argument of how much God knew and even ordained/planned ahead of time. Some Christians believe that, since God knows everything, God knew if you were going to heaven or hell, even before you were born. For this group, since God knows who the hell-bound folks are when they show up, there isn't anything we (or God!) can do about it. Those who promote the idea of double predestination assume hell is probably well populated and accept that as simply how it is.

Lutherans, on the other hand, opted early on for a single predestination approach. In other words, if you trust in what God has done in Christ, God has always wanted you to (after all, Lutherans believe that God wants *everyone's* trust!). Your faith is no accident. It is the work of a God who is working in all of us. But if you don't believe, Lutherans have been unwilling to write it off as destiny. God's commitment to everyone goes deeper than our experience or judgments about the adequacy of other people's faith.

The confessions of the Lutheran reformers said, "The eternal election of God, however, predestination that is, God's ordination to salvation, does not extend at once over the godly and the wicked, but only over the children of God," (Formula of Concord, Article 11:5). In other words, we know what we know about people who trust what God has done in Jesus. We can speak with confidence about the hope and promise that belongs to them. As a matter of discipleship, we are committed to hoping that hell, should it exist, is empty and not full. Our confidence in God's grace for us calls us to hope that God will be gracious with others—even those who are different from or offensive to us. This is not a confidence in humanity. It is a commitment to the grace of God being beyond that which we can define.

    The bottom line is that Lutherans are committed to the belief that trusting God's work in Christ brings life. We live out of that faith and the hope and promise that comes with it. But we are not willing to say "to hell with everyone else." We hope and pray for the best for all people, hoping (some would say "expecting") to be surprised by a God of amazing grace.

For Reflection or Discussion

Look at the following passages from the Bible and take some time to reflect or discuss how these texts relate to the idea that grace for us includes hope for others. Discuss this with others or spend time reflecting or journaling about your thoughts.

» Isaiah 55:1-9
» Colossians 1:15-20

Take time to think about the following questions and then either journal personally about them or discuss them in a group:

♥ What did you think about this chapter? What point or points stand out about it most?
♥ Where have you felt excluded in your life (in any setting – it doesn't have to be religious)? How did you feel? What helped you deal with it?
♥ What kinds of judgment and condemnation have you heard in your circle of relationships? Elsewhere in the media? When you hear things like this, what do you feel emotionally?
♥ What kinds of things could you do in your local setting to be more aware and open to graciousness with people from different faith traditions and backgrounds? How might these embody the belief that God's grace can be for them as well – even though they might think and believe differently than you?

The Jack
Vocation of the Baptized

Perhaps no aspect of the Reformation is more threatening to the previous status quo than the Lutheran notion of vocation. This is the doctrine that teaches that all people can be useful to God's purposes in any place and at any time. There are not "holy" things to do and "unholy" things to do. Because God is concerned about everything and everyone, everything matters and everyone can be part of that.

Before the reformers, vocation was the idea that *some* are called to the work they do, supporting the belief that life was a two-tier system. There were religious people (priests, monks, nuns, etc.) who were called by God to do their work in the church. This was sacred and holy work where people were set apart to live lives that mattered and were viewed as special by both the church and by God. In fact, the word "vocation," which means "calling," is still applied primarily to religious occupations in many parts of the church.

On the other hand, the rest of the people did the ordinary things in the world. Because these roles were worldly, there was no sense that the work was all that important important to God. Unlike the "calling" by God to do religious work, these people were simply cogs in the wheels of the world, taught that their hope was in heaven but that their earthly work and lives provided little of real value.

Martin Luther was raised in this worldview. The son of a miner, Luther was studying to work in church law, an occupation outside the "higher callings" of priestly and monastic life. In the famous story of his deeper commitments to the church, cringing in fear while trapped in a thunder storm, Luther reports that he cried out, "St. Ann, save me and I will become a monk!" Surviving the storm, Luther dropped his legal studies and began to study for the priesthood.

Eventually, Luther discovered that becoming a monk did not alleviate his anxiety about measuring up to God's standards. Both he and his wife, the nun Catherine Von Bora, eventually left the cloistered life and returned to life in the world. When Luther shared his insights with the world, the walls between the sacred and the secular not only cracked, but also came crashing down. When he found out that being a priest didn't help the anxiety he felt about his imperfections, he discovered a bigger truth—God can and does use you anywhere.

The new insight for the church was that God can use people in all occupations and roles to serve as instruments There is nothing more holy than to work as a parent, a farmer, a teacher, or any of the many other roles that people live out in the world. These are all ways that God uses people to contribute to making it work well. God is at work in each and every situation in the lives of people.

The life of faith helps provide meaning and purpose in all places, in all people and in all occupations. The vocation of all Christians is ultimately much the same, regardless of where each person finally ends up doing his or her work, which enables us to demonstrate our love of neighbor and to tell of the God we meet in Christ. Lutherans believe that God can, and does, use a wide variety of people and the work they do to make the world function, not just Christians. But those of us who are among the baptized are "put on notice." We know our lives matter and that God values the work we do. We are blessed to think and act with more intentionality as a result.

Sadly, this foundational belief that all of us have a vocation is still waiting to be fully lived out in the life of the church. Old habits die hard. Deep-seated beliefs have a way of hanging around. Church leaders need to spend more time and energy equipping people to allow all aspects of their lives to be shaped by their faith and the call to be faithful. As they do, the baptized people of God will discover increasing relevance for how their faith informs their daily lives, and how God uses them to make a difference and do what matters. In remembering their baptism they will see both a gift that brings life and a call to join in with God's work.

Because the "calling" of all Christians is to be useful to God in what they do, wherever they are, it is often helpful to consider our lives as having various arenas. We are called to be useful to God in our homes, shaping our children or honoring our parents with our lives. We are called to be faithful signs of God's care in our community, advocating and working for the common good of our neighbors. We are called to be signs of God at work in our occupations, contributing to the ongoing way the world works. And we are called to be faithful in the church, nurturing and supporting each other as people of faith, shaping the church to be God's agents in the world.

The vocation of the baptized frees all of us from the burden of finding that one special thing we can do that is pleasing to God. We are set loose to live our lives and do God's work in all that we do, whether we leave our current setting and go half way around the world or stay home and raise our kids and go to our current jobs. When we recognize that everyone can be useful anywhere, there is great power waiting to be set loose.

For Reflection or Discussion

Look at the following passages from the Bible and take some time to reflect or discuss how these texts relate to the concepts concerning the vocation of the baptized. Discuss this with others or spend time reflecting or journaling about your thoughts.

- » Genesis 1:26-31
- » Romans 12:1-8

There are often four arenas where our lives are framed: home/family; church/faith community; civic/public life; occupation (paid or volunteer). Take time to think about the following questions and then either journal personally about them or discuss them in a group:

- ♥ What did you think about this chapter? What point or points stand out about it most?
- ♥ How does your current action in each of these areas serve God's desire for people to be loved and for a better world?
- ♥ What could you do to be more clear and intentional about serving as God's hands and feet in those settings?
- ♥ What help would you like from your congregation to help you do a better job in each of these four arenas of your life?

The Ten
Priesthood of all Believers

Because God has come to us in Christ and is present and accessible to all who have faith, all Christians have the ability and the calling to serve as priests for their neighbors. Luther's commentary on 1 Peter 2:4-10 is especially helpful here where he states:

Consequently, since He (Jesus) is the Priest and we are His brothers (and sisters), all Christians have the authority, the command, and the obligation to preach, to come before God to pray for one another, and to offer themselves as a sacrifice to God.

This calling to proclaim (share the message of the gospel with others), pray (intercede with God on behalf of the other), and to sacrifice (to offer one's self for the benefit of others) defines the content of the Christian life. In no way does Luther see it as unique to the ordained, but as an essential aspect of what it means to belong to Christ. It is the direct corollary of the idea of vocation that we discussed in the previous chapter, but brings its own unique contribution to the Lutheran message and worldview.

While vocation is about our ability to serve as instruments of God in our daily lives, the priesthood of all believers is about our ability to be a mediating presence between God and the world in which we live. In a sense, vocation is about what we do and say. Priesthood is about where we stand—in between God and others. At any time, any and all of us may be in the place in between, playing the priestly role of going to God (in prayer) or coming from God (sacrifice or proclamation) for the sake of the gospel.

There is a common phrase attributed to Martin Luther that says we are to be "little Christs" for each other. I have given many talks where I ask people to raise their hand if they have heard Luther quoted with that phrase. Inevitably, in a Lutheran crowd lots of hands go up. Lots of people have heard it. In fact, lots of pastors have said it.

The odd thing is that Luther never said it! Luther said we are to "be Christ" for each other (no word "little" inserted before it). When Luther says we are to "be Christ" for each other, this is what he means: Hebrews tells us "there is one mediator between God and humanity, Jesus Christ," (1 Timothy 2:5). While our vocation demonstrates our ability *to be useful* to God's purposes with our own lives, the priesthood of all believers is more focused on *our identity to be Christ* for others—we are commissioned to be Christ's true presence in the settings in which we live and serve as mediators between the God we meet in Jesus and the people and issues we encounter in our lives.

This ability to serve as a mediating presence between God and other people is one of the most powerful innovations of the Reformation. It knocks clergy off the pedestal and levels the field for ministry for and by everyone. Baptism becomes something that unites us with Christ (Romans 6) and reminds us about the power that we all have to minister (with humility as Christ) to others. It is a constant reminder of God's commitment to work through the abiding presence of Christ, which is promised to all who believe.

At St. Mary's Church in Wittenberg, Germany, is an altar that Martin Luther commissioned Lucas Cranach (a painter who used art to communicate religious and theological themes) to paint. The altar has one large panel at the bottom and three smaller ones at the top. I will share more about the bottom panel of this altar in Chapter 7 on worship. For now, we will focus on the three smaller pictures across the top. The panel on the top right shows the priest of St. Mary's Church administering confession and forgiveness. This is a reminder that transformation is an expected part of the Christian life and a healthy reminder in today's world to take the call to renewal and discipleship more seriously.

The other two panels are remarkable in their focus on who they show leading the church.

The top left panel shows a baptism at a font in the church—this is not an emergency baptism in a crisis. Gathered around the baptismal font are a group of people to celebrate the baptism of a recently born baby. Normally, it is our practice that the person who presides at a baptism if there is not an emergency situation would be an ordained pastor. But officiating at the baptism in this picture is Philip Melanchthon, a key leader in the Reformation. Only Melanchthon was never ordained!

The top center panel shows Lucas Cranach's son leading communion around a table where people are gathered in the presence of Jesus. Cranach's son was a soldier who was never ordained, either. Yet he is shown presiding at the meal in spite of the presence of as prominent a pastor as Martin Luther himself. Imagine a church like that, in which laity and clergy all able share leadership and are priests to each other. This is not to say that this to become a free for all or that anyone should simply decide for themselves that they are to do this. This is a communal ministry – one in which we share responsibility in the work of presenting Christ to each other. But it is certainly an imagination stretching idea to think about how we can and should be doing better at this when we are gathered.

To be honest, while the priesthood of all believers is one of the oft-mentioned strong points of our Lutheran identity, there are those who feel like vocation of the baptized is what Luther talked about and that priesthood of all believers (a phrase coined later and which Luther never exactly used) is a misunderstanding of our faith. Luther specifically addressed this issue in his *To the Christian Nobility of the German Nation* in 1520 where he says, "We are all consecrated priests through baptism."

While the actual phrase "priesthood of all believers" was first coined after the Reformation, it is consistent with Luther's trajectory and holds a powerful place in the vocabulary of Lutherans today. It is faithful to our baptismal understanding and it is both helpful and important for our identity in this new day. Our trump cards originated with Luther and other early reformers, but the Lutheran movement was not frozen in time—it continued (and continues) to mature and change.

It is also true that the "priesthood of all believers" is still more theory than practice. In the *modus operandi* for many of us, priestly ministry still belongs more to the ordained than to the whole people of God as it is lived out. While this may simply be put off as reflecting different roles in the life of God's people, the truth is that not everyone needs to be presiding at communion, baptizing new Christians or preaching in the pulpit for us to do a much better job of teaching people of faith to claim and carry out their priestly ministry. Faithful Christians are called to pray, speak and act in priestly ways within the natural flow of their daily lives. It would change how we interact with each other, with neighbors and co-workers, and how we lived with our families in our own homes.

The possibility of new ways of being church is wide open for us. Since all of us can manifest and mediate God's work among us, it is in our DNA, and only our imagination limits the many ways that this can and will be lived out.

For Reflection or Discussion

Look at the following passages from the Bible and take some time to reflect or discuss how these texts relate to the concept of the priesthood of all believers. Discuss this with others or spend time reflecting or journaling about your thoughts.

» 1 Peter 2:4-10
» Revelation 1:4-8

Take time to think about the following questions and then either journal personally about them or discuss them in a group:

♥ What did you think about this chapter? What point or points stand out about it most?
♥ How have you experienced the presence of God working in your life through other people? How have they been Christ for you?
♥ Who do you see regularly in your life (family, work, community, church) that you are praying for? Are there people for whom you should be praying more often? Perhaps consider dropping them a note to let them know you are praying for them.
♥ Who do you know is praying for you? How do you know? Have you thanked them?

The Nine
Life is Sacramental

To understand how Lutherans view the world one must look to Martin Luther's sacramental understanding of life and God's presence within it. It is both connected to Lutheranism's Roman Catholic roots and somewhat distinct from it at the same time.

A sacramental view of the world means that Lutherans understand God to be present within creation. The incarnation of Jesus is the centerpiece of this truth. In the person of Jesus the, "Word became flesh and dwelt among us" (John 1:14). The God who many see as far away and watching us from a distance has chosen to come close to us in Christ. Jesus reminds us of this presence and promises to be with us "always" (Matthew 28:20), whenever "two or three are gathered in his name" (Matthew 18:20), united with us in baptism in "a death like his" (Romans 6:5). For a Christian, life in the presence of God is a 24/7 reality. This promise, revealed in Christ, is not some sort of magic made real in Jesus. It is simply how the world is. God is on the loose – present and at work in the world.

One of Luther's concerns was the preoccupation with magic. In contrast to the view that God is already here and the gospel announces this and declares it so – the church practices at that time implied the priestly power to make God show up. It felt like magic. In the Latin mass, the priest's words were unintelligible to the people in the pews, which made it appear that the church had the power to conjure up the presence of Christ. In fact, the magician's magic words, *"hocus pocus"* are thought to have been derived from the Latin words, *"Hoc est corpus"*, which were used in the mass to announce that the bread had stopped being bread and was now the flesh of Jesus.

The presence of God was distant, and then, through the power of the church, the average person thought that it was manifested in the sacrament of communion. The view was that God was generally watching from above and lived far away and then, in the magic of rituals, could be conjured up and made close. This "magic" actually made the bread stop being bread and become the flesh of Jesus. It made the wine stop being wine and become the blood of Christ. Called "transubstantiation," this explained how God's presence could come to us by replacing reality with the presence of the divine. It was now understood to be Jesus *instead* of bread and wine.

In contrast to this, Lutherans connected sacramental presence to something bigger than just the sacrament itself. Grounded in the word that becomes flesh, the Lutheran understanding of communion did not make Jesus show up. Nor did it somehow replace reality and show Jesus had come instead of what was there already. Rather Lutherans assumed that Christ was already present and that the bread and cup were vehicles to show and announce it in a way promised by Christ. Where does Jesus go to church on non-communion Sundays anyway? Lutherans intentionally chose to say less about how this happens than their predecessors and used the language of "in, with and under" the bread and the wine to describe this (technically known as "consubstantiation"). This understanding meant that God's presence exists *with* reality, not *instead* of it. The result was to emphasize the presence of God in order to announce, acknowledge and experience it. But the goal was also to see the presence of communion as part of the larger real presence of God in the world around us. The goal was to help people see the presence of God, not just in the moment, but also in life.

Ultimately, a Lutheran understanding of sacraments is tied to our understanding of the Word from John 1. The same Word that became human in the person of Jesus is the Word that also called everything else into being. Luther could see God's Word incarnate declaring God's work in the world around him. This enabled him to say, "Our Lord has written the promise of resurrection, not in books alone, but in every leaf in springtime."

The previous chapters all either point to this sacramental view of life or depend on it—a sort of chicken and egg question. You can start in either place, but eventually you get to all of it. Our entrance into the priesthood of all believers and our doctrine of vocation both assume that the God revealed in Jesus is not far off in heaven but rather is deeply involved in the ordinary. The real beauty is found in God's closeness to our world and God's participation in everything.

While it is easy to fall prey to superstition about sensing God's presence and work in the ordinary, it is also important to help people pay attention to seeing God at work in daily life. Ask most of us about the five most precious and holy moments in our lives – places where we sensed God was present and working – and most people will name events and places outside the context of the church sanctuary and worship. They will talk about being present at the bedside of a relative as they died, being in the delivery room at the birth of a child, watching the sun set over the horizon of a beautiful setting, or any one of an almost infinite number of settings and situations. One reason it is so important to immerse ourselves in scripture is to ground our ideas of what we see and hear as we watch for God who is present and at work in the world.

The incarnation is real and regular. Communion is one particular example of a general truth about the presence of God. It is a gift given to us in order to help us to see Christ present in a place God promises to be present. As we share in the presence of Christ in the bread and cup we are reoriented to see that same God in the places we might not otherwise notice. As we encounter Christ "in, with, and under" the bread and cup we, are also confronted by the Christ who is "in, with and under" the stuff of life. The baptized, those who are "united with him" (Romans 6), live a life that is identified by this reality as a 24/7 identity. Yet, the sacramental nature of life is not limited to being manifested only in and by the faithful. It is true wherever God is at work—in people of Christian faith, other faiths, and no particular faith—but only through the eyes of faith will it be seen and acknowledged for what it is.

For Reflection or Discussion

Look at the following passages from the Bible and take some time to reflect or discuss how these texts relate to the idea that life is sacramental. Discuss this with others or spend time reflecting or journaling about your thoughts.

- » Psalm 95:1-7
- » Job 12:7-10

Take time to think about the following questions and then either journal personally about them or discuss them in a group:

- ♥ What did you think about this chapter? What point or points stand out about it most?
- ♥ Think about the five most precious times in your life that you treasure as "holy." What are the stories about them and where did they happen? How many took place outside of the church sanctuary?
- ♥ When you want to spend time with God during a typical weekday, where do you go? If you don't have such a place or places, what can you do to create or discover one that
- ♥ What settings bring a sense of wonder and awe or awareness of God's presence and reality for you? Why do these places or settings work for you?
- ♥ Consider the last few days. Where did you see God at work in your daily life?
  - » What blessings did you receive (be sure to take a moment to give thanks)?
  - » What blessings did you share (be sure to take a moment to rejoice)?

The Eight
Worship is Horizontal

Over the last few decades, church groups of various backgrounds have been involved in a variety of conflicts over worship and how to do it. Should it be traditional and remain consistent with the style and content used for decades or even centuries? Or should it adopt a variety of contemporary elements and styles to make it more fresh and appealing to today's people? This conflict has often been labeled "worship wars."

Lutherans have not been immune to this stress. Many congregations have had deep divisions over changes in worship. Others have made changes more smoothly and have agreed to offer more than one style—most often one labeled "traditional" and the other labeled "contemporary." Of course these labels are somewhat relative. Some sing hymns, use a guitar and call it contemporary. Others sing more updated songs but use an organ to accompany and still consider it traditional. Still others have made major modifications in the liturgy (the order of worship in which people participate) and use country, pop, rock and even heavy metal music to lead worship.

Underneath this variety of responses about style lies an even more important issue. Where is God in all this? The answer to this question is not as simple as it may seem and the content of worship is often significantly changed based on the underlying assumptions.

Much music in the broader Christian community is oriented toward singing to a God who dwells in heaven and watches from a distance. The goal of worship is to open up the people present to the Holy Spirit who connects us to a God who is somehow "other" than the community. This emphasis often uses language of lifting up prayers, raising our songs, a God who dwells in heaven above, etc. In many of these traditions, communion is celebrated infrequently and is seen as a memorial—a reminder of what God did in Christ when he walked the earth and went to the cross for us. While these traditions are faithful worship expressions within the framework of the people who practice them, they are not Lutheran. They seek to center and refocus a community of faith to remember God's coming in Christ and to offer praise and prayers to a God who remains "other."

Contrast this with Lutheran theology. In our framework, the God who has come close in Jesus still continues to come close to us. This is both a daily thing (remember, life is sacramental!) and a focus of our worship life, through which we seek to celebrate the God who has come into our midst. Our preaching, our music and our actions are all changed by this reality.

Two key examples may help here. Remember St. Mary's Church in Wittenberg, Germany? In Luther's day it was where the ordinary people went to worship. There was another church at the castle where the more well-to-do and powerful folk attended. In Chapter 5, we looked at the top three panels Cranach painted on the altar that sits in this church. We are now going to look at the rest of the altar. The bottom panel shows a picture of the congregation gathered for worship with Luther delivering the sermon from the pulpit. The effect of this preached word is not to tell people about the Jesus who went to the cross, but to show them that same Jesus in their midst. In this painting, the crucified Christ can be seen manifesting his presence right in the midst of the gathered people of faith. This is Lutheran preaching at its best. It doesn't just inform people about Jesus. It helps them actually see the crucified and risen Christ right there among them. Worship that is horizontal does not seek to tell us about a God who dwells up in heaven. The focus is to encounter the incarnate God in the midst of the gathered community.

The second example is how Lutherans and some other sacramental churches understand communion. Although there are some nuances to communion in these traditions, one key is that we understand communion to be about the "real presence" of Christ. As we eat the bread and drink from the cup we hear the words, "The body of Christ, given for you" and again "the blood of Christ, shed for you." These words announce that in this bread and cup we encounter the real presence of Jesus. We are encouraged to respond to that by saying, "Amen," which means, "this is true" or "I believe it" or "let it be so." In other words, communion announces that, as we gather for worship, Jesus is not somewhere else to be praised and remembered from a distance. Jesus is in our midst to be honored and praised right here. Communion servers declare this truth to each person as they distribute the sacrament. Those receiving communion reiterate this word by saying, "Amen" in response to the good news of Christ's presence.

These two things, preaching and communion, stand at the center of Lutheran worship as a people formed in a word and sacrament tradition. In more and more Lutheran congregations we are seeing not only preaching each week, but an increase in the frequency of communion; many congregations now celebrate communion at every weekend worship gathering. Good preaching and the sharing of communion help people encounter the living Christ in their midst.

All of this influences how Lutherans plan and lead worship. Songs and liturgies that emphasize lifting our voices to be heard by a God in heaven don't feel quite right. Words that simply tell us about a God who did something long ago, and simply share principles for living based on what happened and what the Bible says, seem somehow lacking. We hunger for words that help us honor the God who dares to come into our midst as we gather. We long for lyrics in songs and hymns that help us see and relate to the God who is only arm's length, and not an eternity, away. And we hope to leave worship with eyes that not only see God in ways that refresh us, but also with eyes to see that same God present with us and working around us all week long.

Lutheran worship is not vertical, as if God is in heaven waiting for us to arrive some time after we die. Lutheran worship is horizontal and celebrates a God who is incarnate and who has come closer than we might think.

For Reflection or Discussion

Look at the following passages from the Bible and take some time to reflect or discuss how these texts relate to the idea that worship is horizontal. Discuss this with others or spend time reflecting or journaling about your thoughts.

» Psalm 98 and Psalm 100
» Matthew 18:15-20

Take time to think about the following questions and then either journal personally about them or discuss them in a group:

- ♥ What did you think about this chapter? What point or points stand out about it most?
- ♥ In the worship services that your congregation provides, where is Christ's presence most clear for you? Least clear?
- ♥ If Luther's premise that preaching should not just tell people about Jesus but show them the crucified and risen Christ in their midst, what in preaching best helps you "meet" Jesus rather than simply hear about Jesus?
- ♥ What ideas do you have for leaders in your congregation to consider that would make Christ's presence in the midst of your worship clearer and more experiential for people?

The Seven
Love the Bible Without Worshiping it

One of the phrases that characterized the Reformation was *sola scriptura* or "scripture alone." To be fair, the Lutherans had a list of these "alone" things so they weren't quite alone, but they were priorities that stood at the core of their message.

Martin Luther translated the four Gospels into German while being held in protective captivity in Wartburg Castle. When he came out and published them he wrote an introduction called, "What to Look for and Expect in the Gospels" to help people read scripture with a bit of priming. These folks had not read much before, had poor instruction about the basics of their faith, and now were going to dig into the Bible. It was too big a task to have them do without a little advice. In fact, for Luther, understanding the Bible meant correctly knowing the gospel.

Early in his introduction he tells these new Bible readers that, "scripture has a wax nose, you can bend it anyway you want." 500 years ago, Luther knew that interpretation was as important as scripture. A faithful reader would need to know the gospel in order to make sense of the Bible. Proof texting and overly legalistic thinking would not allow scripture to speak with a living word that would present the reader with an encounter with Jesus. Although it was long before modern fundamentalism was even conceived, Luther was already doing a preemptive strike on fundamentalist, idolatrous understandings of scripture and taking verses out of context to selfishly use them as weapons.

Instead, scripture was seen as "the manger in which the Christ child was laid." The point of scripture is the gospel encounter with a God who spoke the world into being, who became present in the midst of life as "the word made flesh" and who continues to speak as a living word that shapes and gives life in the present. This is not just a God who spoke in the past. That means that faithful reading of scripture does not always give the Bible the last word, for it is a living word. But it does give scripture the first word; it is a place to start, focus our attention, and from which to listen for what God is saying to us today.

For today's Lutherans, reading scripture takes on many dimensions. It is a faithful witness to our encounters with the God who came to us in Jesus. It is the "source and norm" of our tradition, a place to start the conversation. But because Lutherans believe that the word is alive and not dead, the word that is in scripture is but one expression that came in Christ and continues to speak. Reading scripture allows people to recognize God's voice in a place where Christians have long agreed that God's voice can be heard—the Bible. But we also read the Bible, not to find the last word, as if the Bible were an answer book to every question life brings. We read the Bible to become familiar with God's voice in order to be able to recognize that same voice as the living word, which continues to act and speak today.

Most of us have people in our lives with whom we have a deep and abiding relationship. If I talk to my mom or dad on the phone, I don't need them to tell me who they are. I have heard them speak so many times and know their voices deep in my being. When they say "hello," I know exactly who is on the other end of the phone line. Our conversation moves our relationship forward as we continue to talk and share bits and pieces of our lives.

Time in scripture is like time with close friends or family. It allows us to get to know the God who is witnessed and speaks to us in the Bible. It is a place to meet Jesus, the incarnate Word of God, and to recognize who he is. It is not the end of that relationship but the beginning. From our encounter with Christ in scripture we are better able to see Christ in the world around us and in our lives. This Christ, the living Christ, is the one we follow.

Our Jewish cousins have a tradition known as Talmud. Talmud is the ongoing teaching of the Torah, the Jewish scriptures that are the canon of their faith community. In Talmud, the ideas and stories of many Jewish traditions and ideas are collected to illuminate how what was said can help us make sense and come to life in our time and place. Jewish rabbis will tell us that their view of scripture is that when we dig into something significant, the Torah always gets the first word. It is the place to start. Then the community of faith wrestles from that starting point in order to move forward and discern a word for today. It is not just bringing the same thing forward. It is grounding the conversation in God's word, and then letting that unfold and shape ideas that help us make sense of our world today.

Lutherans understand that scripture is not the last word about God. It is a starting point and provides a first word. God is still alive and working, speaking and guiding. So we start with scripture, we watch and listen for the presence of Christ, and then we wrestle with that word and the issues facing us together. The result? New ideas, new directions and new life. Only a Bible that witnesses to a living word allows Lutherans to take it seriously, but not worship it. It is where we start, but we always end by following the living Christ.

For Reflection or Discussion

Look at the following passages from the Bible and take some time to reflect or discuss how these texts relate to the idea that we love the Bible without worshiping it. Discuss this with others or spend time reflecting or journaling about your thoughts.

- » Psalm 1
- » John 1:1- 14

Take time to think about the following questions and then either journal personally about them or discuss them in a group:

- ♥ What did you think about this chapter? What point or points stand out about it most?
- ♥ What are your current bible reading habits? How do you decide what to read? How often do you read (be honest!)?
- ♥ What do you like most or best about the Bible? Why is it important for you?
- ♥ What barriers do you experience to spending more time and becoming more familiar with scripture? What do you think would help you deal with these?
- ♥ The Bible is filled with all sorts of good stuff but is also sometimes confusing and even conflicting for us when we read.
    - » How do you make sense of the Biblical story as a whole?
    - » What do you do about troubling or confusing passages?
    - » Where could you find support or help to get a better handle on these?

The Six
Perfection is not the Point

There are a lot of different takes on what happens when you become connected to Jesus. Some churches teach that the goal of the life of faith is holiness; faith calls you to stop being a sinner and to live a life free from sin. This is not the approach most Lutherans take.

One of the phrases that Lutheran pastors still say is the Latin phrase, *Simul justus et peccator* (using a little Latin still makes us sound smart, doesn't it?). It means that we are "at the same time justified and sinner." Often you will hear a Lutheran say we are at the same time "saint and sinner." What this means is that, even though we trust in Christ and receive righteousness before God as a gift, the reality of our sinfulness is a given part of our existence. We can't escape it. It is always there. In fact, the Lutheran understanding of sin has less to do with what we do than the condition in which we live out our lives.

There is a T-Shirt I received as a gift from the Old Lutheran Gift Store. When I wear it, the graphic on the front raises a few eyebrows. On the surface, the message sounds so counter to the dominant Christian message. It has a picture of Martin Luther and a logo that looks like the label on a beer bottle. The "brand" of the beer is "Sin Boldly Lager." It is based on a quote from Martin Luther, who once said, "Be a sinner and sin boldly, but believe and rejoice in Christ all the more boldly."

Lutherans at our best are not preoccupied with perfection, nor are we overly bothered by our imperfections. Don't misunderstand this—it is not an excuse for laziness or lax ethics or morality. What we do, and our reasons for doing, matters greatly. But, at our best, we have somewhat given up on trying to be perfect. That is part of the freedom and release that Christ gives us. We are loved in spite of our imperfections. We don't have to measure up in order to be loved. God has declared us righteous and we know this through our faith. This declaration is enough; we don't have to fix ourselves to be blessed by God.

This was a radical departure from the dominant teaching in Luther's time, which had placed a heavy burden on people. Sins were viewed as huge problems and no one was worthy to encounter God in eternity without being fully cleansed of them. Sin was understood primarily as the individual failings and shortcomings that each person had. Confession and repentance provided a system by which people could go erase or compensate for their sins. But, all sins had to be worked through. Anything not dealt with in this life led to time in purgatory, where people could end up spending hundreds of years to work off all the sins still not dealt with prior to dying. Often, church leaders abused this belief, allowing people to be coerced out of time and money in the hopes of releasing people from their struggles sooner. Only a perfectly sin-free person could eventually enter the kingdom of heaven. Fear was rampant and the church teachings added to the anxiety in many ways.

Luther's efforts to confess everything and perform acts of penance nearly drove him, and the priest to whom he all too often confessed, crazy. Obsessed with his sinfulness and the weight of the imperfections he bore, Luther tried everything to cleanse himself of his sins. It was a never-ending, unfulfilling process.

Luther's great insight came when he realized that God's love is the one thing that makes us worthy. We are not perfect, but we are perfectly loved. God declares us righteous in Christ as a gift. Luther didn't have to be perfect to be right with God.

Likewise, he understood from his previous attempts to avoid and repent of sin that he was just stuck being imperfect. He was also faced with tough choices, all of which had some sinful aspect or collateral damage, even the choice that seemed the best one possible at the time. For many years this resulted in a tentative stance toward life, filled with indecision and second-guessing. Nothing seemed good enough for God.

Rather than being paralyzed by the imperfection of the options, Luther's freeing insight resulted in the message, "There is no perfect option—period. Everything involves sin in some way—period. So choose the best choice you can, imperfect though it may be, and give it your all. Sin boldly, but believe and rejoice in Christ more boldly!"

This is one of the great gifts of Lutheran teaching. It is realistic about ambiguity. In a complex world, Lutherans recognize that there are not often simple solutions. Our teaching about social issues can be nuanced and realistic. Our leaders can weigh options and use insight, wisdom and courage to wrestle with and pursue hard decisions. Knowing that life offers few clear choices, we are free to jump into the fray and get messy as we work to serve as the hands, feet and voice of Christ. We don't have to find the perfect solution or have all the answers in order to get involved and be helpful.

It is also true that this can be hard to live with. In an either-or world, where we prefer easy answers and simple solutions, living with complexity and ambiguity can feel a bit unnerving. Only in the broader picture, painted by the gift of grace, does this make sense. Living under the pressure of the law, where getting it right is the point, the fact that life is ambiguous can be terrifying. This was Luther's experience. It is grace that allows us to live within the ambiguity of real life.

This is not a directive to be sinful. It is an acknowledgement of the fact that we are; rejoice that we are important to God and useful to God anyway. It is the freedom of being loved by God and, therefore the willingness to offer ourselves as we are, in order to join in with Christ's work for the sake of the world.

For Reflection or Discussion

Look at the following passages from the Bible and take some time to reflect or discuss how these texts relate to the idea that perfection is not the point. Discuss this with others or spend time reflecting or journaling about your thoughts.

- » Romans 3:21-31
- » Romans 7:14-25

Take time to think about the following questions and then either journal personally about them or discuss them in a group:

- ♥ What did you think about this chapter? What point or points stand out about it most?
- ♥ How do you experience yourself as BOTH good and bad? Where do you struggle between the reality of being sinful and the reality of being in God's image? Do you feel more good or bad most of the time? Why do you think that is? Is there something that would help you recover more of a sense of the aspect (sinner or saint) that you miss most often?
- ♥ We live in an "or" world but bring to it an "and" theology. What examples of this either/or divide do you see most often in our society? How do you feel about the consequences of this?
- ♥ How can Lutheran Christianity's ability to hold together things that sometimes seem to be in opposition be a gift to our world today?

The Five
Response Is Freedom and Gratitude

One of the Achilles' heels of Lutheranism has often been our attitude about action. Since much of the Reformation debate focused on the need to start with, and emphasize, Christ's grace as gift, Lutherans have been accused by some of their opponents of forbidding, or at least discouraging, good works. There were even jokes about Lutherans, whose confidence in their salvation by grace was proven by their commitment to never do any good work (just in case they started to trust in their own goodness).

Much of this was because, in trying to reform a system that emphasized what people had to do in order to get right with God, the focus of the Reformation was on the basic truth that people couldn't do anything to get themselves right with God. Along with that came the good news that they didn't have to anyway. The work of Christ offered righteousness and new life as a free gift. The result was a polemic that rightly emphasized grace, but appeared to discount or dismiss good works.

Nothing could be further from the truth. To emphasize this, the writers of the Augsburg Confession (a document that laid out the most organized attempt to explain the reformers beliefs and concerns) wrote in Article VI, "Also they teach that this faith is bound to bring forth good fruits, and that it is necessary to do good works commended by God, because of God's will, but that we should not rely on those works to merit justification." In other words, people of faith necessarily produce good results, not because they have to, as if they are obeying the rules, but because it simply is who they are in Christ. It is as natural for people of faith to produce good works as it is for an apple tree to produce apples.

All of this emphasizes that the Lutheran understanding of faith is that God always goes first. It is not our actions to please God that initiate a change in our relationship with God or our status before God. It is God's actions in Christ that initiates that. God goes first.

This understanding of life is ultimately very freeing. In Galatians 5:1 Paul says, "It is for freedom that Christ has set us free." Since God has done this on our behalf, we are freed from the burden of having to accomplish this for ourselves. We are free to do pretty much anything. There are no "rules" that set appropriate requirements for our actions as people of faith.

At the same time, this freedom, in the life of the Christian, is grounded in the presence of Christ. Because we are free, we need no longer live out of anxiety, self-doubt, selfishness, or any of the other things hold us captive. Claimed by the love of Christ, we are free to love our neighbors and serve as instruments of God.

How we use that freedom is shaped by gratitude. Faith tells us that God in Christ does the necessary work. Gratitude is the natural response to any gift, especially for one as powerful as this. The core insight of Lutheran teaching is that the first response to God is not working harder to please God. Instead, it is thankfulness that we don't have to.

The result of this is a gracious and freeing stance toward life. Lutherans are able to serve free of the worry that what they do will not be enough or will not work off their indebtedness. Lutherans are free of any sense of entitlement and the attitude that comes from believing you are in charge of your own destiny. Lutherans can be filled with a joyful engagement of life and the world based in gratitude and sharing the love they have received from God, knowing that there is plenty more where that came from.

George Forell wrote a book entitled *Faith Active in Love* (American Press, 1954). It may be the best title ever placed on the cover of a book about the Lutheran take on faith. Because we are loved, and the God who loves us needs nothing from us, the love we receive from and feel toward God is redirected toward our neighbors, taking on a life of meaning and purpose that is offered freely and with thanksgiving.

It is no accident that, because Lutherans don't have to do anything, so many do something. Lutheran Services in America is the largest network of social services and ministry in the United States. In addition, Lutherans are involved in building homes, housing the homeless, feeding the hungry, mentoring kids in schools and doing all sorts of amazing things that make a real difference in the world around them. In addition, we are caring neighbors, loving parents, and diligent employees. We are free to do these things knowing that we don't have to do anything in particular. That frees us to do what matters most to God and to our neighbors. Having to do nothing also brings the freedom to do lots of amazing things in response to God's grace in Christ.

For Reflection or Discussion

Look at the following passages from the Bible and take some time to reflect or discuss how these texts relate to the idea that our response is freedom and gratitude. Discuss this with others or spend time reflecting or journaling about your thoughts.

- » Psalm 107:1-9
- » Galatians 5:1-15

Take time to think about the following questions and then either journal personally about them or discuss them in a group:

- ♥ What did you think about this chapter? What point or points stand out about it most?
- ♥ Think about the freedom that is yours in Christ. How do you exercise that and experience that during a typical week?
- ♥ What holds you captive? How can you take time to allow grace to free you from it? Who has God given to you in your life who could help?
- ♥ If gratitude is a key to living a joyful and gracious life, for what are you most thankful? How do you express that to yourself and others during the average day or week? What could you do to improve this aspect of your life?
- ♥ Thank you notes and cards that are written by hand have become a bit of a lost art for many. Yet almost no one receives a handwritten thank you without feeling a bit special. Who do you need to take time to thank with a note? How could you take a few moments each month to reflect on the month and add writing thank you notes to your routine?

The Four
Faith Forms the Church (It's about people!)

There is a phrase that states, "There is no salvation outside the church." It is well intended and, in the right context, can provide a helpful insight. However, while this thought can be helpful if one has a healthy and broad-minded attitude, it can be quite exclusive and damning if one thinks in the narrowest of terms.

During the time of the Reformation, the church was quite hierarchical. Power rested within the church, and those whose positions rested at the top of the church's structure dispensed that power. The head of that church, the Pope, was seen as Christ's mediator within the world. Like the phrase in the opening paragraph of this chapter, with an open and healthy attitude this might be a helpful thought. But in the context of power and corruption it was a dangerous one. The church held the keys to salvation and the church's leaders were able to dispense it as they saw fit. Rather than salvation coming as a gift from God and received through faith, that faith was seen as coming through the church and being dispensed to the people. A saving faith was the property of the church to distribute or not.

Contrast this with the way the reformers understood how the church came into being. The Augsburg Confession describes faith's freely-justifying benefits in Article IV. It explains how faith happens through the ministry of the Word and the work of the Holy Spirit in Article V. It describes the impact that faith has in the life of people whose faith frees and transforms them to produce good works as fruit of faith. *Only after all of this do the reformers even mention the church.*

Even more telling than this is how they describe the church. The church is defined as the "assembly of believers." In other words, people who believe are gathered together by God's common work in their lives and become the church. For the church to come into being, faith has to be present in people. The church does not have a corner of faith and then pass it out to some and not to others as it sees fit. The church is built on the work of Jesus and the faith of those who have come to know and trust in that work. These people gather for shared worship, support and the joining in with God in that work.

The biblical basis for this can be found in 1 Peter 2:4-5 which says, "Come to him, a living stone, though rejected by mortals yet chosen and precious in God's sight, and like living stones, let yourselves be built into a spiritual house, to be a holy priesthood, to offer spiritual sacrifices acceptable to God through Jesus Christ." This text views the church as a people, not as an institution. The church does not dispense faith to its people; the church is made up of people who have faith. Instead of the church hierarchy controlling people and holding power over them, the church's leverage over people is reduced. There is a new equality and freedom present in the life of the church when people are involved and included in leading the church.

This same mindset shapes how Lutherans (and many Protestant Christians) interpret the confession of Peter in scripture. Jesus asks what people are saying about him. He then focuses the conversation by asking the disciples what they think of him. Peter speaks and says, "You are the Messiah, the Son of the living God." (Matthew 16:16, NRSV). Jesus affirms this and responds, "On this rock I will build my church." Traditional Roman Catholic teaching has emphasized the person of Peter as the rock and has seen this as establishing the papacy as the cornerstone of the church. But Lutherans and other Protestants do not think that Jesus is referring to Peter the person, but to his statement of faith. It is faith in Jesus as Messiah that is the basis for the church.

A wider involvement of people in discerning the direction for the church bears out the impact of this. Lutheran gatherings include laity and clergy working together. Bishops are elected by these gatherings and are to work more as servant-leaders in the church, rather than as authorities over it. Social statements and teachings, expenditures of funds, and decisions impacting all sorts of things are not made apart from the life of the people by a only a powerful few. At our best, they involve the people of faith who are the living stones that make up the church.

For Reflection or Discussion

Look at the following passages from the Bible and take some time to reflect or discuss how these texts relate to the idea that faith forms the church (it's about people). Discuss this with others or spend time reflecting or journaling about your thoughts.

- » Acts 2:37-47
- » Ephesians 2:19-22

Take time to think about the following questions and then either journal personally about them or discuss them in a group:

- ♥ What did you think about this chapter? What point or points stand out about it most?
- ♥ The old children's song "Here is the Church,…" ends with the line "see all the people." If people are the church, how does your congregation emphasize people over things like buildings, programs and money?
- ♥ How do the building, programs or money get in the way or distract us from focusing on people?
- ♥ A part of the emphasis on people as the basis of the church is about where we invest our energy. How could your congregation invest more time and energy in people to equip them to be the church?
- ♥ What would help you personally better own the idea that you are the church, even when you are away from the building?

The Three
We Have an Ecumenical Heart

When pastors are ordained, diaconal ministers and deaconesses consecrated and associates in ministry commissioned (a list of things that are NOT Lutheran Trump Cards!), they are asked a set of questions about the work they will do and the way they will do it. It is a promise of faithful leadership and a willingness to remain faithful to the Lutheran movement's understanding of the gospel as one begins his or her ministry as a part of the whole catholic church.

One of these questions is about teaching and leading in accordance with the Augsburg Confession. It is about doing ministry in a way that stays true to the core commitments of the authors of that work and to the central insight that grounds the whole thing (Article IV and "justification by grace through faith."). These core convictions, already discussed in earlier trump cards above, define the center of who we are.

But, sometimes Lutherans forget the real reason for the Augsburg Confession and the convictions that underlie its message about the church. We have already said that faith constitutes the basis for the church. People of faith are the church and the church is where faithful people are. More than a concrete institution, this view of the church is of an organic movement that is too big to be contained under the definitions used to identify most human institutions. That limitation includes those who bear the label "Lutheran." While Lutheran Christians are part of the church, Lutherans do not have a corner on being the whole church.

In fact, the reason the Augsburg Confession was written in 1530 was to make one last good-faith effort to avoid the church being split into fragments. The reformers really wanted to stay part of the Catholic Church. Because they only believed that there is one church anyway, the best way to embody that truth was to stay connected and work for the unity of the church. The Augsburg Confession was written to outline the commitments shared by everyone in the church, as well as those points where disagreements remained and proved to be divisive. But the goal was *not* to start a new church, something they didn't believe to be possible, by definition. The goal was to preserve and embody the true unity of a church that was more faithful to the grace made real in Jesus.

To be honest, Lutherans have, throughout the years, often forgotten this aspect of the Augsburg Confession. The Augsburg Confession, written to try to heal divisions, began to function more like the Declaration of Independence—a code of commitments that defined why we stood apart. The attitude hoping to unify and heal the church was lost. The Augsburg Confession became a doctrinal litmus test to which allegiance could be sworn as opposed to a witness set in the hope of finding common ground and bringing a more gracious and unified church into being.

The way this can be understood in today's world happens at two levels. First, the Evangelical Lutheran Church in America (ELCA) has been a bridge to unification within Lutheranism itself in this country. Comprised of multiple strands of the Lutheran tradition that were divided by national origins, geography, piety and other factors, the formation of the ELCA brought together most of the previous Lutheran strands in this country. To be fair, that work is not complete as two major segments of Lutheranism in the United States have not connected: the Lutheran Church, Wisconsin Synod and the Lutheran Church, Missouri Synod. Both of these strands have remained committed to a more doctrinal and less ecumenical understanding of Lutheranism and how the Augsburg Confession functions. Likewise, some within the previous strands have chosen to leave. Many have left over ecumenical partnerships, especially those with the Episcopal Church. More recently, others have left over disagreements about the church's position on including gay and lesbian people in leadership. But those who have left have done so because the theme of this chapter is true. The strand of Lutheranism that has come together to form the Evangelical Lutheran Church in America (ELCA) is committed to a bigger picture of what the church is and who it includes and that is exciting to some and scary or offensive to others.

A second level has happened specifically in the area of ecumenical relationships. The ELCA has been committed, from early in its history, to working with others and formalizing agreements to do this work. These agreements, known as full communion, have meant that the church has agreed to share ministry and leadership across denominational lines. Early agreements were heavily focused on doctrine, especially with regards to issues like communion. It has grown to work for a broader basis of shared work and, as of this publication, includes agreements with the Episcopal Church, Presbyterian Church (PCUSA), the Moravian Church, the United Church of Christ, the Reformed Church in America and the United Methodist Church. Lutheran ministers can preach and teach in congregations from these traditions and their ministers can do likewise in Lutheran congregations. To be sure, there are protocols for such work to happen, but it can and does result in real work happening. In addition, a Joint Declaration on Justification was issued in partnership with the Roman Catholic Church in 1998.

All of this is making more and more sense to many people at the local level. Lutheran congregations and their members work within all of these full communion agreements and participate in ecumenical ministerial associations that include joint work and ministry across all sorts of lines, which are far broader than those formally ready to be confirmed at a denominational level. Food pantries feed the hungry with Pentecostals serving in Lutheran basements. Soup kitchens cook meals with Lutherans cooking in Catholic kitchens. Pulpit exchanges result in Lutheran preachers sharing sermons in Baptist pulpits.

In the end, this card may be one of the biggest gifts given to the whole church by Lutherans. As a group that originated in ways that brought pain and fragmentation to the body of Christ, something in the Lutheran heart longs for healing and unity. This church serves as a bridge to the one true church, being more and more visible within the world in which we live. It is slow, hard work, and far from completed. But it is clear that, within the Lutheran psyche, there is a desire to help the church live as one church in ways that are real and make a difference in how we join in God's work in the world.

For Reflection or Discussion

Look at the following passages from the Bible and take some time to reflect or discuss how these texts relate to the idea that we have an ecumenical heart. Discuss this with others in a group or spend time reflecting or journaling about your thoughts.

» Ephesians 4:1-6
» John 17:20-26

Take time to think about the following questions and then either journal personally about them or discuss them in a group:

- What did you think about this chapter? What point or points stand out about it most?
- The Evangelical Lutheran Church in America has many "full communion partners." These are denominations with which we have taken an extra step to affirm that we are part of something bigger than ourselves. Go to www.elca.org and type "full communion partners" in the "search" window to look up who these partners are. Which ones have congregations near you? Do you have any relationship with them?
- Many congregations do local ministry in partnership with congregations from other Christian traditions and even other non-Christian faiths. What does your congregation do in partnership with other faith communities in your area?
- What do you know about the faith traditions of others who live near you? What other faith traditions have congregations near you? Is there a group at your congregation who could make an effort to meet others and find out more about them?
- If someone were to ask you what you think about Christians from other traditions, what would you say in response to them? What about people of faiths other than Christian – what might you say about them?

The Two
We Are Always Watching for Change

There are two ways to consider reform. One is to reflect on the past, discover or decide what was wrong, and then fix it. In this method of reformation, the goal is to get things right, and the assumption is that, once we analyze and clarify these things, the new answers we articulate will be correct. They are of enduring value and are new claims of truth and correctness. To be honest, within many confessional traditions, this understanding of reform exists. The faithful statements lifted up in confessional writings are understood to be litmus tests for all future work. There was an old way that was wrong. We fixed it. Now we are right. This understanding of reform is *not* at the core of our tradition.

At our best, the Lutheran faith is *semper reformandi*, a Latin phrase that means "always reforming." Vibrant reformation traditions are best understood and function well when they do not see a past point as terminal, as a final truth to be defined for all time. Rather, living confessional traditions see previous confessions as faithful efforts to share truth and make sense of the gospel. They also serve as pointers to the central things that matter most to them, and continue to serve as a foundation to guide us with important cues about how to share faithfully in our own time and place.

For those of us in the Lutheran tradition, this means that looking at something like the Augsburg Confession reminds us of foundational beliefs like God, sin and God's coming to us in Jesus. It points to a central truth that is the core of the tradition: the belief that the God we meet in Jesus is ultimately gracious, and that faith is a gift that allows us to see that truth. The reformers applied that gracious commitment to various aspects of the Christian life, the church's life and to the world in which they lived in the 1500's.

This is the Lutheran method. We continue to articulate the basic understandings about the goodness of God, the reality of sin and the gracious gift of God's coming to us in Christ. We stand on the reality of grace as the hinge on which our view of the world turns, and to faith as the gift that allows us to see and trust that this is true. But the real work of a movement like ours is to *continue* to ask the questions and provide answers as to how this impacts the Christian life, our life together as a community of faith and the way we understand the world in which we live.

There are two key reasons as to why we need to continue to be open to change:

» The world is changing and calls for new ways of seeing and articulating faith and faithfulness.
» God is active and alive, always on the move. This means that we have to be watching, as God is doing a new thing. To settle for the old answers may be to miss what God is up to.

Because we live in a new time, a new place and face new issues, to be confessional is *not* to regurgitate the answers of the reformers, but to stand on their shoulders and wrestle with how to answer these same questions, along with new questions, today.

This has allowed the church to oppose slavery, ordain women and gay and lesbian people, and repent of Luther's writings that slammed the Jews in his time. Grounded in scripture, but listening for the voice of God speaking still today, we dare to change in ways that seem good to us and are led by the Holy Spirit. Change is not easy, and not all decisions are clear and perfect. We have said above that we live in an imperfect world with few perfect options. Just as we are free to "sin boldly" as individuals, so the church must also dare to "sin boldly" as it navigates a changing world and seeks to bear witness to a God who continues to be with us through thick and thin.

In the end, a confessional leader may even articulate a faithful answer that seems at odds with some of the answers from 1530, *and still be faithful and helpful in our time*. This is because, in the end, this tradition of being a Lutheran Christian is a movement and not a destination. It is committed to gracious relevance in the lives of its people and the world in which it functions. To walk in the footsteps of the reformers is to give thanks for their work and the grace of God they helped the world to see. Honoring them is more than simply quoting their answers to the people of their time, it is trying to reframe and share the good news of God in Christ in our time as well.

For Reflection or Discussion

Look at the following passages from the Bible and take some time to reflect or discuss how these texts relate to the idea that we are always watching for change. Discuss this with others or spend time reflecting or journaling about your thoughts.

- » 2 Corinthians 5:11-17
- » Ephesians 4:20-24

Take time to think about the following questions and then either journal personally about them or discuss them in a group:

- ♥ What did you think about this chapter? What point or points stand out about it most?
- ♥ What are the biggest changes happening out in the world in the area where you live? How has your congregation intentionally changed to adjust to these?
- ♥ Over the last ten years, what are the biggest changes (good or bad) that your congregation has experienced?
- ♥ If you grew up in the church, how is the faith and congregational life you have now different from that of when you were a kid? How is it the same? What do wish the church had changed but still seems pretty much like it was when you were a kid?
- ♥ If you are newer to the church, what aspect of church life is most puzzling to you? Least connected to your daily life? What would you like to see the church consider in order to be clearer and more helpful now?

Conclusion

Well, that's it. Our suit of cards is complete. You have enough cards in your hand to make a good play in almost every situation. The key is being familiar with what's in your hand, and knowing how to play your cards wisely and in ways that are helpful.

Remember that this is a Lutheran *suit*. These are our trump cards. Other faithful traditions have more cards to offer. We don't have the whole deck! We are *part* of the church and glad to be working as God's people with many others. There are even strands of Lutheranism who would argue with some of the ideas put forth in this book. In the end, these other traditions have received much from us and some of their cards look familiar to us. But they also have their own unique things to share and we need to see our suit as a contribution to the church as a whole as well as be open to learning from others. Remember to use this in the spirit of always being open to change (it is one of our cards!).

You may find yourself in a situation where someone says something or does something that you find challenging. Or you may find yourself in a place where someone is hurting and needs a word of hope and grace. We know that we have something to offer that might help start a conversation that opens up new possibilities. The cards we have in our hand may provide a chance to say something helpful and begin a dialog where there may have previously just been a monolog.

As we finish, let's remember the cards we're playing with:

- **Ace:** There is no way to God (period)
- **King:** Jesus reveals that God is love
- **Queen:** Grace for Us Includes Hope for Others
- **Jack:** All the baptized have a vocation
- **Ten:** The priesthood of all believers
- **Nine:** Life is sacramental
- **Eight:** Worship is horizontal
- **Seven:** Love the Bible without worshiping it
- **Six:** Perfection is not the point
- **Five:** Respond with freedom and gratitude
- **Four:** Faith forms the church
- **Three:** We have an ecumenical heart
- **Two:** We are always watching for change

It is important to remember that, while the face cards are foundational and extremely useful, all of the cards have value. Every idea in this list may just be what you need to reflect on, speak or act on in any given situation. Just as when you play a card game, you look to draw certain cards, depending on the game and what you have already sitting in you hand; so it is with the cards of faith. Every card in our suit will be useful at one time or another. Remember to think about what you encounter and which parts of our faith connect most naturally to provide something helpful. And remember the call to be a person of grace. Our ultimate goal is to be both gracious and helpful – not to merely overwhelm people with different viewpoints.

A healthy congregation will find ways to help people learn to know the cards in their hands, and practice using them when the church is gathered. It is not enough for the pastor to mention these, or even to elaborate on them during a sermon (although pastors *should* be doing that, too!). Simply hearing about these things is not enough. In fact, there is probably very little in this book that people who regularly attend a Lutheran congregation haven't already heard several times. But hearing is a small part of competence. Equipping people means helping them apply ideas and practice using them together. Healthy church life should look less like an audience listening to a lecture and more like an interactive lab session with people experimenting with ideas and practices to see how they work. We gather for practice for just a few hours each week; we have to make good use of that time. The rest of the time we are elsewhere and life goes on.

Make a list of these ideas and phrases. This is about more than memorizing lines for a play. It is about internalizing the ideas, and owning them as central to your life of faith and to your identity as a Christian. Grab a friend and talk about them. Think about times in the last few weeks where you saw a news story, heard someone say something at work or in your family, or wondered about something in your own life. Then look at the ideas in our Lutheran suit of cards. Which ideas speak to the things you thought of? What words of life and hope can you say to address the situations you remember seeing or being a part of? Help each other to think about this and enjoy the chance to practice with someone who is as committed to growing in their faith as you are.

In the end, our ability to share our faith, in ways other than the confrontational front-porch evangelism that we have experienced too often, will depend on developing a more gracious message and being fluent enough to know that we don't need to shove the whole deck of cards down someone's throat. Knowing what we have to work with and what might be helpful in a given situation means we can do a better job of loving and supporting each other in the church. It also means that we can be more confident and helpful as Christians as we talk to our families in the evening, share life with co-workers around the water cooler or participate in the public life of our communities. Ultimately, be glad that you have been invited to join with Christ at work in the world in ways that share God's love and make the world a better place in which to live.

For Reflection or Discussion

The end of this book is also a chance to begin some new practices. Reflect about the following questions and also think about who you could approach to help adjust your congregation's practices to better reflect and equip people for the concepts you have been reading about and discussing here.

» Who in your congregation (members as a whole or leaders in particular) would benefit from being in a discussion about the trump cards we carry as Lutherans? How could you help start such a conversation?
» What ideas could you consider as ways to help your congregation could change or improve its practices in order to let people both learn more and practice more about the trump cards Lutherans have at our disposal? Consider ideas that could bring about changes or adjustments to practices in:
  » Worship life
  » Equipping and educating people
  » Outreach, witness and evangelism
» Which of the trump cards do the people in your congregation need to pay extra attention to right now? How could you take time to emphasize that in a way that would be helpful?
» Think about how your leaders spend their time. How much of it is simply shaped by generic concerns of being an organization? How much of it focuses on the unique gifts and identity we bring as Lutheran Christians? Should there be an adjustment in the focus and if so, what ideas do you have for that?
» What would help you as an individual to get more help and practice digging into the Lutheran trump cards in ways that make you more confident and capable of living and sharing your faith as a Lutheran Christian?